Mental illness

Vanora Leigh

WAYLAND

Talking Points series
Alcohol
Animal Rights
Charities – Do They Work?
Divorce
Genocide
homelessness
Mental Illness
Slavery Today

Editor: Alex Edmonds
Series editor: Alex Woolf
Designer: Simon Borrough
Consultant: Kaaren Cruse

First published in 1998 by Wayland Publishers
Ltd, 61 Western Road, Hove, East Sussex,
BN3 1JD, England.

© Copyright 1998 Wayland Publishers Ltd

Find Wayland on the internet at
http://www.wayland.co.uk

**British Library Cataloguing in Publication
Data**
Leigh, Vanora
    Mental illness – (Talking points)
1.Mental illness – Juvenile literature
I.Title
616.8'9

ISBN 0 7502 2179 8

Printed and bound in Italy by G. Canale &
C.S.p.A., Turin

Acknowledgements
The author would like to thank organizations
such as SANE and MIND for their help in
compiling this book. Special thanks go to
Daniel Leigh, Bill Roberts and Vicky Sharman
for additional research in the UK and USA.

Picture acknowledgements
Bubbles Photo Library: 8 (Frans Rombout), 11
(Loisjoy Thurston), 16, 43 (Loisjoy Thurston),
48, 54 (Peter Sylent). Eye Ubiquitous Picture
Library: 53. Getty Images Ltd: 5 (Frank
Herholdt), 7 (Penny Tweedie), 10 (Bruce
Ayres), 17 (David Stewart), 18 (Frank
Siteman), 19 (Paul Edmondson), 20 (Andy
Sacks), 23 (Laurence Dutton), 28, 29 (Julian
Calder), 30 (Bushnell/Soifer), 31 (Steve
Taylor), 33 (Bruce Ayres), 35 (Tom Raymond),
40 (Connie Coleman), 42 (Penny Tweedie), 46
(Bruce Ayres), 47 (Ziggy Kaluzny), 49 (David
Harry Stewart), 50 (Jon Riley), 51 (Frank
Herholdt), 52 (Eric Tucker). Richard and Sally
Greenhill: 13, 24, 44. David Hoffman Picture
Library 4, 9, 14, 26, 27, 32, 39, 41, 57, 58,
59. Hulton Getty Picture Collection: 28.
Impact Photos Ltd: 6, 12, 21, 22, 34, 38, 55,
56. Chris Schwarz Picture Library: 15, 25, 36,
37, 45.

Contents

What is mental illness?

Today we talk quite openly about sex, about AIDS, about drugs, about violence, about divorce, about death. Nothing is taboo anymore … except for one subject. We still don't talk about mental illness. Once there was a time when cancer and tuberculosis weren't discussed, when people thought there was something shameful in getting those diseases. That's how it is with mental illness now.

The days when people suffering from mental illness, the 'insane', were locked away in Victorian mental institutions may have gone, but we still sweep mental health problems under the carpet. The result is that those affected remain socially, if not physically, isolated and apart.

When you are mentally ill, problems can grow out of proportion. It becomes hard to think clearly. You often want to shut yourself away and not talk to anyone.

Mental illness, or mental distress as some people call it, has always been more difficult to sympathize with than physical illness, because it's harder to see. And it's something we like to believe happens to other people, not to us. Yet mental illness affects a great many of us, directly or indirectly, at some point during our lifetime. One in ten adults and up to one in five children will suffer from a mental illness severe enough to need professional assistance. We probably all know people whose faces are strained with anxiety, who have a friend or relation who is unstable, depressed or deluded. And sadly, it could happen to you.

Can you remember the last time you felt really unhappy? Perhaps you'd got bad grades in your exams or had a row with your best friend. You may have cried and shut yourself in your room for a few hours. Then, a day or two later, everything began to look brighter again.

You realized you could re-sit your exams; you called your friend and you both apologized. You were sad, but now you feel better again. Imagine, then, a sadness that doesn't go away after a few days, but persists for several weeks or even longer. You cry a lot; you shut yourself in your room for days on end; you refuse to go to school or to talk to anyone; you stop eating. Your worried parents call the doctor and he says that you are suffering from depression.

Talking point

"Globally, in developed and developing countries alike, mental illness and health-damaging behaviours exact a tremendous toll in human suffering, evident in the distress and despair of individuals and the anguish of their families ...The tragedy is even greater because much of it could be avoided, were we to commit ourselves to applying what we know, and learning what we don't, about prevention and treatment.'

The views of the former USA President Jimmy Carter and Rosalynn Carter, writing in the foreword to the World Mental Health Report, first published in the USA and the UK in 1995.

Do you feel that you really understand mental illness? What do you think could be done to the improve knowledge and understanding of both sufferers of mental illness and other people?

Sadly, mental illness takes the joy out of everyday life for people of all ages and backgrounds, throughout the world.

Illnesses of the mind

Depression is a mental illness affecting the mind and emotions. Like a physical illness, a mental illness needs treatment – for some people just a short course of tablets and/or counselling, for some a stay in hospital, for others, just talking to friends and counsellors.

As people get older, their mental health may deteriorate. They can become confused and forgetful and may develop Alzheimer's disease, one cause of senile dementia.

And just as there are many different types of physical illness, so there are many different mental illnesses. Doctors often differentiate between what are called 'serious' mental illnesses and other forms.

Schizophrenia, manic depression and some cases of severe depression fall into the first category. Sometimes you'll see them described as psychotic disorders because sufferers may lose touch with reality and have delusions or hallucinations.

Less serious mental health problems are frequently referred to as neurotic disorders. They include depression, anxiety states, phobias, panic attacks and eating disorders, such as anorexia and bulimia.

Other types of mental health problems are caused by diseases which affect the brain. The best known is probably Alzheimer's disease, which is one of the causes of senile dementia in some older people.

Know what you are talking about

Mental illness should never be confused with mental handicap or learning disability. A learning disability is caused by damage to the brain, either before birth, due to an accident or in early childhood. As a result the brain does not develop as fully as it should. Some learning disabilities have a genetic basis, as in Down's Syndrome. A learning disability, which is the most common disability in the world, is not an illness and cannot be cured.

Who becomes mentally ill?

By 2020 mental illness will be the most common illness in the developing world, according to the World Health Organisation in 1997. Even today, mental illness is as common as heart disease and three times as common as cancer. Just as some people are physically stronger than others, people have different psychological strengths and weaknesses. These are determined by our personalities, past experiences and the genes that we inherit. Some experts now believe that just as we inherit our physical characteristics from our parents and grandparents, mental illness may run in families, in the same way that heart disease or cancer does.

There are times when we all feel that there is nobody to talk to. Sometimes these feelings of isolation become so strong that people become depressed.

Stress and depression

All of us will find ourselves under pressure at times, such as when we take exams or start a first job; all of us will experience distressing events such as death and perhaps divorce. These events can leave us feeling anxious and depressed for a time.

With extreme depressive or stress-related mental illness, these feelings are so intense that they make it difficult for the person to cope with life. When this happens it's often said that someone has had a 'nervous breakdown'. Doctors seldom use this term, saying it is too vague, but many people who have suffered with a mental illness think it is appropriate.

When you are studying for exams, the pressure to do well can even make you depressed for a while.

Do we really understand mental illness?

Despite the fact that all forms of mental illness are on the increase throughout the world, most people still know very little about it. What they do 'know' is often based on prejudice and ignorance. Think of the insulting words used to describe the mentally ill, terms which are also used as insults in the playground and in the street. Many people gain the little knowledge they have about mental illness from newspapers, books and films, where the mentally ill are often labelled 'mad'. As a result, people with mental illness lose their identities and are seen as as social misfits or even as highly dangerous. The fear of violence from the mentally ill has been fuelled by the reports of very disturbed people – many suffering from schizophrenia – who have been released from hospital and then attacked members of the public.

Name-calling in the playground often consists of insulting words, used by the ignorant, to describe the mentally ill, words which are based on prejudice and ignorance.

Talking point

'Look at the slang for mental institutions: booby hutch, bug-house, funny farm, loony bin, nut hutch. Bugs are low on the evolutionary scale; hutches and farms are places where animals are kept; a bin is for rubbish. This kind of language grew out of a culture in which the mad were banished or confined.'

Author Blake Morrison writing about the continuing prejudices against mental illness in *The Independent on Sunday* in 1994.

Why do you think people continue to use such insulting language? Is it because they think mental illness is funny, or is it because they regard sufferers with contempt or fear?

Across the world, people still confuse mental illness and mental handicap, and few understand the differences between a serious mental illness and the more common forms such as mild depression and anxiety. They also fail to recognize that in the majority of cases mental illnesses can be treated and stabilized, even if a cure is not possible.

Many people who are stressed or over-worked are afraid to admit to symptoms of strain and depression in case they lose their job.

This sort of ignorance makes it almost impossible for someone who has suffered with a serious mental illness, such as schizophrenia, to find any form of work, which creates even more problems. Even those who have suffered from minor mental illnesses are reluctant to tell potential employers because they fear they will be discriminated against. Often, people in work who are suffering from stress or depression are reluctant to seek treatment, in case their employer discovers they are 'mentally ill'. Can you imagine the outcry if people with a physical illness or disability were treated in this way?

Case study

Yvette is a 30-year-old journalist from Paris. When her company announced it was making large-scale redundancies she feared her job would be one that would go. It didn't, but life didn't get any easier.

'So many people had gone – down-sizing they call it – that each of us was doing the jobs of several people. It was bad enough when we were all at work, but if someone was ill or on holiday everything fell to pieces. People who had been good, friendly colleagues became irritable, it was a case of every man and woman for themselves.'

Yvette was suffering from stress but didn't like to admit this to anyone, even if her behaviour showed she was obviously under pressure. When Yvette did see her doctor she prescribed tablets for her and told her she should stay away from work for a month. 'I knew I should do what she said, but I was terrified I'd lose my job,' she says.

Yvette was dismayed when people she regarded as friends failed to understand her illness. 'One told me he didn't know how someone as intelligent as me could break down like I had. He said some physical activity, like a long walk or scrubbing the kitchen floor would make me feel better! If only!'

Stress can become unbearable and lead to a full mental breakdown.

Types of mental illness

One of the problems of understanding the term 'mental illness' is that it is used to describe many different conditions, with a whole range of causes and effects. Over the next eight pages we will look at several forms of mental illness. They are all different, but have two main factors in common: they all cause distress, not just for individual sufferers but for entire families, and they are all on the increase.

What is anxiety?

Modern life can be extremely stressful and anxiety is often unavoidable. The cause of the anxiety may be something specific like a family feud, or it may be what is sometimes referred to as 'free-floating' anxiety – a persistent stream of worries and anxious thoughts about life in general, particularly future events over which we may have no control. This kind of disabling anxiety can produce the most distressing physical symptoms, known as panic attacks. Here the build-up of anxiety can lead to feeling faint, a racing heartbeat and difficulty in breathing. Around two-thirds of people who see doctors about severe anxiety states will improve or recover. If anxiety does persist there is a risk of other common psychiatric problems, such as phobias and mild depression, developing.

Feeling fearful

Phobias are exaggerated fears related to particular situations. Common ones include a fear of open places (agoraphobia) and fear of confined spaces (claustrophobia). A register compiled by USA university researchers in 1997 lists 314 phobias. These include agyrophobia – fear of crossing the road; anthophobia – fear of flowers and plants; chinophobia – fear of snow; and mythophobia – fear of telling lies. Closely related to phobias are obsessions – repetitive, usually unreasonable, thoughts and patterns of behaviour that keep occurring for no good reason.

Modern life isn't easy, and sometimes the pressures and problems may just seem too much to cope with.

What is dementia?

Of all the diseases associated with ageing, dementia is the one most feared by the elderly and their relatives. It has been described as a 'living death', the personality of the individual sufferer being completely destroyed, while physically they may remain quite fit.

What actually happens?

Dementia occurs when the cells of the brain die more quickly than in normal ageing. People become confused, behave oddly and lose track of time and events. Most people lose a small part of their memory as they grow older, but dementia is not just caused by old age. It involves specific changes in the brain caused either by Alzheimer's disease or by a blood vessel disease called multi-infarct dementia, brought on by high blood pressure.

Around one in ten people over 65 have some symptoms of dementia, rising to one in four in people over 85. Alzheimer's disease is thought to have a family link – one in three sufferers has a close relative who also has the disease. Dementia occurs equally across all groups in society and does not appear to be linked with class, race or geographical location. Often sufferers lose their ability to hold a conversation, read or shop. These symptoms of dementia are particularly distressing for relatives of sufferers to see.

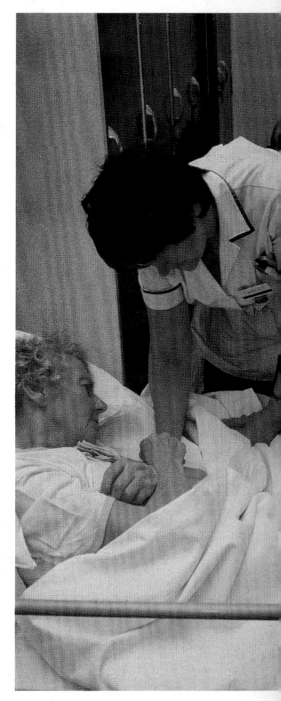

Dementia is sometimes called a 'living death'. It currently affects one in ten people aged over 65.

What is depression?

Depression is sometimes called the 'common cold of psychiatry' because it's the most widely experienced mental illness. It's thought that as many as one in five adults will suffer from some form of depression in their lifetime, but no one can be sure of exact numbers. This is because many cases, possibly 70 per cent, go unrecognized and untreated.

When you are depressed you often wonder what the point of life is. Days seem hopeless and bleak, you have no energy and you can't sleep. Some people even have suicidal thoughts.

What does it feel like to suffer from depression?

Symptoms of depression include tearfulness, feeling useless and unwanted, not bothering with friends, anxiety, poor concentration, lack of energy, loss of appetite and sometimes suicidal thoughts. Often sufferers can't sleep, or they wake up very early and are unable to get back to sleep. We all have unhappy periods in our lives when we feel 'depressed' or fed-up, but most people usually manage to cope and bounce back in a fairly short time. In clinical depression, negative feelings are so intense that life looks hopeless and bleak. These feelings don't ease with time but become worse. Without treatment, such as a course of anti-depressants or counselling, the depression can last for weeks or months.

A matter of degree

Doctors tend to describe depression in terms of degree: mild depression, the most common form, which often occurs after an upset, when you feel low but can still cope with everyday life; moderate, when

What is a psychotic illness?

People use the expression 'psycho' to mean someone who is rebellious and ignores society's rules, but what does psychotic really mean? People who develop a psychosis have a serious mental health problem because their illness means they cannot tell what is real or unreal. They may hear voices speaking to them which sound quite genuine, or they may develop irrational beliefs and fantasies. When someone is in a manic phase of the illness, they become over-active and cheerful. They may lose their normal inhibitions, spend money recklessly and make decisions they later regret. They may even believe themselves to be somebody they are not, and are often so full of energy they exhaust those around them. Writers and artists who suffer from manic depression claim they are usually very creative in a manic phase.

you are unable to function as well as normal; and severe depression, a chronic condition which can prevent sufferers from getting out of bed, going to work, looking after children and thinking clearly. People with severe depression are at risk of committing suicide. The risk of drug, alcohol and solvent abuse is also increased.

Manic depression

People who suffer from manic depression experience swings of mood which are much more extreme than normal mood swings – from blackest depression to wild excitement. Episodes may last for several months, with gaps between in which sufferers are usually well, perhaps even for several years. Much rarer than depression, manic depression often starts around the age of 30 and affects one person in 200. Unlike depression, it is a psychotic illness (although some people with severe depression do develop psychotic symptoms).

People who develop a psychotic illness lose touch with reality. They may hear voices, voices that may tell them to kill themselves.

15

What are eating disorders?

Anorexia nervosa is an illness that leads to severe weight loss and bulimia nervosa is a related condition that combines over-eating with deliberate vomiting. Both are characterized by a fear of being fat. Unlike someone on a diet trying to lose weight, people with anorexia become obsessed with dieting to such a degree that it rules their lives, and they are even capable of starving themselves to death.

Like anorexics, those with bulimia also suffer from an exaggerated fear of becoming fat and have often been overweight as children. They binge on food, then make themselves sick or take large quantities of laxatives. Unlike an anorexic, someone with bulimia may not look underweight and so the problem may go unnoticed.

People with eating disorders like anorexia or compulsive eating become obsessed with food – how to avoid it or how to increase their intake.

Compulsive eating means eating much more food than your body needs, well past the point of satisfying any hunger. A person who regularly over-eats may not even taste the food. Food is used in this way as a 'comfort' when someone is anxious or worried, but it can lead to being seriously overweight – and there are resulting health problems linked to obesity.

Who suffers from eating disorders?

Around 90 per cent of people who suffer from eating disorders are girls and young women. Older women, children under ten and some boys and young men have also been affected, but in far smaller numbers.

Anorexia nervosa tends to run in families, with 10 per cent of sisters of sufferers developing the illness. Anorexia usually starts in the middle of the teenage years.

Although eating disorders are primarily a Western problem, they are a major problem in South and Central America, too. Argentina may now have the highest rate of anorexia in the world. A study has shown that 29 per cent of girls at secondary school in Argentina have eating disorders. Of this 29 per cent, 9 per cent had anorexia or bulimia.

Talking point

Dr Mabel Bello, an Argentinian and director of the Association for the Battle against Bulimia and Anorexia in South America, once said, 'It [bulimia] is becoming a major health problem. There are cases of girls as young as seven who stick their fingers down their throats and vomit because they want to look like the models and stars.'

The media is often accused of making girls believe they should look a certain way by promoting very slim models and actresses. Can we blame the media for the increase in bulimia and anorexia?

Wherever you look in today's magazines and on television, the message seems to be ' If you don't look like this, you're a loser'.

What are personality disorders?

Doctors use the term 'personality disorder' to describe problems of behaviour which are due to an individual's personality being damaged in some way, perhaps by an emotional or psychological upset during childhood.

Mad or bad?

The best-known category of personality disorder is psychopathic disorder. This term describes the most difficult and damaged people, whose behaviour is likely to cause problems to others. This is abnormally aggressive or seriously irresponsible behaviour, by people who appear unable to feel guilt or consideration towards others. Unfortunately, people with psychopathic personality disorders cannot be successfully treated, and some psychiatrists feel that the only 'treatment' possible is to keep them in a secure place if their behaviour becomes dangerous.

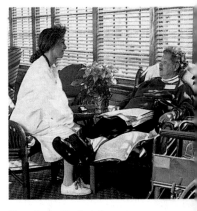

People suffering from a physical illness rarely encounter prejudice, but the opposite is true for those with a mental illness such as schizophrenia, which is misunderstood and feared.

What is schizophrenia?

There are few disorders, mental or physical, that are as misunderstood and feared as schizophrenia. The most common myth about the illness is that sufferers have a split personality (the word schizophrenia means split or shattered mind), with behaviour that swings dramatically between normal and dangerously disturbed. This is not true.

Schizophrenia is a psychotic mental illness. Sufferers lose touch with reality – they see, smell or feel things that don't exist, hear threatening voices and some may start believing that people are plotting to harm them or bugging their conversations. These feelings of persecution are called paranoia. This odd behaviour can be frightening to witness, but imagine how terrifying it is for sufferers themselves.

Reality not myth

There have been several much-publicized attacks on members of the public by severely mentally ill offenders. Many of them were in community care schemes and were schizophrenic. This has only increased the fear and stigma surrounding the illness.

Although so often portrayed as 'homicidal maniacs' in the press, the majority of people experiencing a schizophrenic episode are usually considerably disabled by it – lethargic and afraid to go near other people. They are far more likely to harm or even kill themselves than others.

Who becomes schizophrenic?

Around one in 100 people will develop schizophrenia at some point in their lives, but a quarter will only have the one episode. Others have recurrent bouts of the illness. Schizophrenia can run in families. Like depression, schizophrenia affects people from all countries, cultures, back-grounds and walks of life.

A growing problem

According to the the World Mental Health Report of 1995, by the year 2000 there are expected to be over 24 million sufferers from schizophrenia in the less-developed countries of the world. In China alone, an estimated 4.5 million people suffer from schizophrenia. Less than 2 per cent of them are hospitalized. Another 3 per cent live on their own, and less than 4 per cent are found on the streets, in nursing homes or in prison. Over 90 per cent live with their families, more than double the number who do so in the United States.

Hearing voices is one of the symptoms of schizophrenia.

What are the causes of mental illness?

People once thought that mental illness, particularly severe mental illness, was caused by demonic possession. Surprisingly, such beliefs have not disappeared completely. In 1997, British anthropologists, working in the Caribbean country of Haiti, discovered that what the local people called 'zombies', or 'the walking dead' were in fact people suffering from mental illnesses such as schizophrenia or brain damage. These people had wandered away from their communities, and their lack of will and memory are characteristic of what is called the 'zombie condition'. Even in developed countries such beliefs are not unknown. A recent study at a modern psychiatric clinic in Switzerland revealed that a third of the 343 out-patients, who described themselves as religious, believed that evil spirits lay behind their assorted mental problems. Not surprisingly, doctors today do not share that opinion!

Modern medicine has done much to ease the suffering of the mentally ill, but we still don't have all the answers or treatments that are needed.

Still looking for answers

Over the years, medical research has discovered probable causes and treatment for all kinds of mental illness, but these investigations are far from complete and experts are not always in agreement. For instance, we still don't know for certain what causes that most common of mental illnesses, depression. It seems it's not one, but several factors working together which cause this and other forms of mental illness.

Causes for concern

Many experts now believe that depression, particularly severe depression, may be caused partly by changes in the brain, particularly a shortage of

Talking point

'Parents sometimes dismiss their child's depression simply as bad behaviour. It is very hard for them to admit that their son or daughter is suffering from a mental illness.'

Peter Wilson, Director of Young Minds, the National Association for Child and Family Health.

Does it surprise you that some parents would obviously prefer to believe their child is badly behaved, rather than acknowledge that the child is genuinely ill? Why would parents not want to admit their child had a mental illness?

serotonin, a chemical which regulates mood and emotion. It's similar to the body being short of insulin in a person suffering from diabetes.

Some think that this chemical imbalance is due to inherited brain abnormalities, others that it is triggered by stressful events. One theory is that the two could be linked – that some people's genetic make-up makes them more prone to developing a mental illness like depression, which can then be triggered by emotional traumas (shocks). These sorts of 'shocks' can include bereavement, divorce, redundancy, bullying at school and at work, and long-term stress and worry caused by poor housing, lack of money or overwork. Certain childhood experiences, such as a parent dying, are also believed to make some people more susceptible to depression.

Many physical illnesses can also trigger depression. In women, depression has been linked to the menstrual cycle, the menopause and childbirth. In modern industrial societies about half of new mothers experience mild mood changes lasting from a few hours to a week or two. The more serious condition, postnatal depression, which occurs in about 10 per cent of new mothers, can last for weeks, or even years.

Poor housing and lack of money and opportunities can lead to long-term stress and depression.

Experts now believe that mental illness can run in families. Traumatic childhood experiences, such as losing a parent, can also make people more likely to develop a depressive illness.

Inherited problems

In 1995, a World Mental Health report stated that depression runs in families. There is equally strong evidence, however, that childhood experiences, such as a loss of a parent, can make people more vulnerable to depression and that losses experienced in adulthood can bring on depression.

Unhappy families

Hereditary factors seem to play a strong role in the development of manic depression and schizophrenia. More than two-thirds of identical twins of people with manic depression also develop the illness at some point in their lives. By contrast, about only a fifth of non-identical twins will develop it. Within sufferers' families, some 10 –15 per cent of first-degree relatives (parents, children, brothers and sisters) also develop the illness.

Most of the suggested causes of depression also apply to manic depression, and both genetic and external stress factors are again thought to play a large part in the development of schizophrenia. About one in five sufferers has at least one relative who also has the illness. Those relatives whose genetic make-up is closest to that of the sufferer are more likely to develop schizophrenia themselves in the future – it's been estimated that the child of a parent with the illness runs a one-in-eight chance of developing it.

The brain in focus

Another clue to the cause of schizophrenia comes from special pictures of the brains (brain scans) of people with schizophrenia, showing that their brains have certain physical and chemical abnormalities. These could be inherited, or the result of drugs being used to treat the illness, but some experts believe that they occur in very early life, perhaps due to complications at birth or a viral infection. They are thought not to cause problems until the brain matures in early adulthood.

Triggering an attack

Although they may not always agree, most doctors believe that many people develop schizophrenia, as with depression, after a particularly important life event, such as starting college, having a baby or moving to another country. According to some sufferers, schizophrenia is a frightening thing to live with. Hearing voices can be like experiencing your thoughts as if they're coming from outside your head. Delusions can give you a fixed belief in something, even though common sense tells you it can't be true. Hallucinations can be as severe as seeing a metal paperclip turn into a huge insect, or being watched by strange, alien-like creatures. Symptoms can get so bad that people black out.

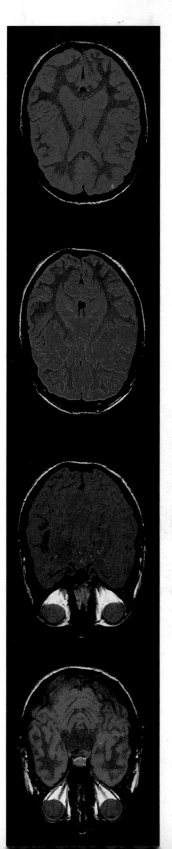

This scan shows a healthy brain, but brain scans of people with schizophrenia have shown certain physical and chemical abnormalities.

Drugs

For a small proportion of sufferers, recreational drug use seems to be definitely linked to the onset of schizophrenia. LSD (acid), Ecstasy (E), amphetamines (whizz/speed) and cannabis (hash/dope) are believed by some experts to trigger schizophrenic episodes. They may bring on some of the symptoms, or make people who already have the illness worse.

Drugs are also linked to other mental health problems. Long-term use of amphetamines, for instance, can cause paranoia and mental confusion, while heavy users can also suffer from severe depression. People already suffering from depression who use cannabis may find the depression intensifies. Long-term use of cocaine and crack can result in paranoid psychosis, and long-term use of Ecstasy may increase the risk of severe depression and mental illness in later life.

Lots of people enjoy drinking, but heavy, prolonged drinking can result in serious mental illness as the drinker gets older.

A drink too many

Heavy drinking over many years can also trigger mental illnesses such as depression, as well as damaging the nerves and brain. Wermicke's encephalopathy is a brain disease which develops suddenly, often after a heavy alcohol 'binge'. Sufferers see double, lose their balance and become confused. Even with treatment, this disease may progress to permanent brain damage and a dementia-like condition, with loss of memory and learning ability. This permanent problem is called Korsakoff's syndrome, after the Russian doctor who first described it.

Addictions

Solvent or inhalant abuse, such as glue-sniffing, which is linked to the onset of some mental illnesses, is not only a problem in the West. It is one of the worst drug addiction problems in Mexico, where an estimated three in every 1,000 people aged between 14 and 24 use inhalants on a regular basis. Serious solvent abuse has also been found on Canadian Indian reserves and amongst Australian Aborigines. In Chile, an estimated 3–5 per cent of children aged 8–15 from poor backgrounds are addicted to glue-sniffing.

Two other kinds of brain damage result from heavy drinking. One is a mental illness similar to schizophrenia. The other is due to generalized shrinkage of brain cells which causes a kind of dementia, called alcoholic dementia.

The shrinking brain

The brains of Alzheimer's disease sufferers, examined after death, have shown several abnormalities, but the causes of this disease are still not fully understood. Overall the brains are small and shrunken because the disease has killed off many brain cells. At the moment, most experts agree that it is easier to say what does not cause Alzheimer's disease than what does, though there is thought to be a hereditary link.

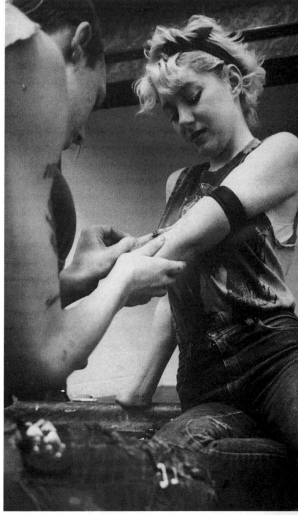

Nobody yet knows what effects drug-taking has on the mind. Even short-term use can cause mental health problems.

Case study

Sara's most precious possession is an old, rather tatty, leather jacket. It doesn't fit, but is rarely off her back. The jacket belonged to her brother Peter. Two years ago, when he was 20, Peter killed himself.

'You learn to live with the pain, but it never goes away,' says Sara. Her widowed mother's distress is as acute now as it was two years ago when the police called at her quiet, suburban home outside Sydney, Australia.

Peter had been living away from home for three years after the death of his father. A previously unremarkable but likeable boy, he had started staying out with friends, taking drugs, and eventually he left the small firm where he was training to be a carpenter. Then he became violent towards his mother and she told him to leave.

'He'd been treated in the psychiatric ward of the local hospital a couple of times,' says his mother. 'He'd collapsed at his flat. I didn't recognize him, he was shouting and ranting. I blamed the drugs he'd been taking.'

When Peter met his mother for lunch he was very depressed. 'He hinted that he'd like to come home, but I knew I couldn't cope with him,' she says. 'I wished then that he could have come back with me, I wish I had let him now, but I honestly couldn't have coped. He said he wasn't managing very well, his medication didn't suit him, he obviously felt frightened and alone.'

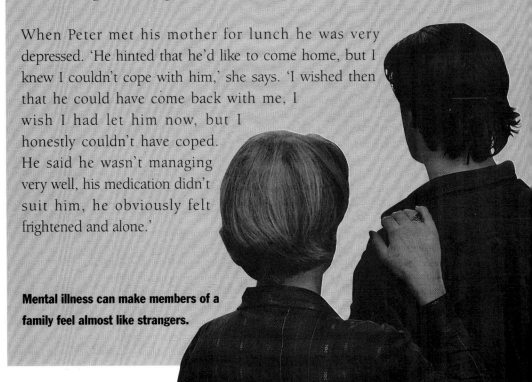

Mental illness can make members of a family feel almost like strangers.

People suffering with a mental illness may find themselves alone when families can't cope with their behaviour.

Peter told his mother he was returning to the local hospital to see if the doctors would re-admit him. Less than an hour later he was found by staff at the hospital in a small, unused side room. Peter had hanged himself.

'He wasn't dead,' says Sara. 'It would have been better if he had been. He never recovered consciousness. He was kept on a life support machine for three weeks. Mum and me went to sit with him every day but he never even opened his eyes. The doctors told mum he was brain dead and she agreed the machine should be switched off. Sometimes I don't think we'll ever stop crying.'

Treating mental illness

When cruelty was the 'cure'

In the past, the mentally ill were punished rather than treated. In Europe in the Middle Ages they were sometimes burnt as witches, while those who escaped this fate were imprisoned in asylums, often chained up like dangerous animals, beaten and forced to undergo harsh, often cruel, 'treatments'.

One of the most infamous asylums, the Bethlehem Hospital (known as Bedlam) in London, started housing 'lunatics' – the old word for the mentally sick – at the beginning of the 15th century. A contemporary inventory revealed that the first six inmates were kept subdued by a fearsome collection of manacles, chains, padlocks and two pairs of stocks. This was thought normal at the time. Throughout the 15th and 16th centuries, 'care' for the mentally sick consisted of forcibly confining them and whipping them to drive out evil spirits.

By the 17th century starvation was a recognized form of treatment. So, too, were bleeding, vomiting and purging. Attacking the body to control the mind was a medically approved method of treating mental illness. The more seriously disturbed were force fed, imprisoned in what was called a 'strait waistcoat' and sometimes permanently chained up. Inmates at

Outside the West there are far fewer medical facilities and staff to help the mentally ill.

Who will care?

In a World Mental Health report, published in 1995, it was stated that the United States had more than 42,000 fully-trained psychiatrists, plus 60,000 psychologists and 75,000 psychiatric nurses for a population of 260 million. In comparison, in Nigeria there are 60 psychiatrists and several hundred psychiatric nurses for a population of 100 million. In China there are three mental health workers for every one million citizens, while Fiji has just one psychiatrist. In Malaysia there are 40 psychiatrists and 800 nurses for a population of 15 million.

Bethlehem were also humiliated, with visitors allowed to come and 'bait' them for fun. Although the conditions appear inhuman to us today, they were not thought so at the time.

Reform

Thanks to campaigns by reformers working for the humane treatment of the mentally ill, conditions in asylums all over Europe were improved during the 19th century. But cases of dreadful neglect have still been reported in recent times. In the early 1980s the world was stunned to hear about conditions in a pyschiatric hospital on the Greek island of Leros. Here, the majority of patients were kept naked and food was put in a single bucket in the middle of a room. There was no toilet.

Although we still do not have a complete understanding of the causes of mental illness, there have been significant improvements in treatment for many disorders in recent years. A cure may not be possible for some conditions, but the aim today is to control symptoms or help sufferers cope with them and regain a better quality of life.

The most common treatments, often used in combination, are drugs and 'talking' treatments – counselling and psychotherapy. Occasionally more drastic treatments, such as electro-convulsive therapy (ECT) and psychosurgery, are used in cases of manic depression and depression which have not responded to other forms of treatment. It's important that the treatment suits the individual as well as the illness.

Taking the tablets

There are a huge number of drugs available for the treatment of mental illness. Doctors today rarely prescribe tranquillizing and anxiety-reducing drugs like diazepan (trade name Valium) because past experience has shown these drugs to be addictive.

Antidepressants used in treating depression are quite different from tranquillizers and are not generally believed to be addictive. Some experts disagree and say that many new drugs have caused withdrawal symptoms when people have stopped taking them. Although some of the older types of antidepressants, such as tricyclic drugs, used since the 1950s, continue to be prescribed, they have been overtaken in popularity by the Selective Serotonin Reuptake Inhibitors (SSRIs). These drugs came into use in the late 1980s and the best known of the SSRIs is Prozac. Acclaimed as a wonder drug on its launch in the United States, it has been described as 'plastic surgery for the personality'. It is estimated that it is now being prescribed at the rate of 650,00 prescriptions a month in the USA. People prescribed antidepressants must remember that they take time to become effective – sometimes several weeks.

Refusing the tablets

Not everyone is in favour of using drugs for depression. Unpleasant side-effects can include nausea, increased anxiety and suicidal tendencies, rashes and disturbed sleep. Many people prefer sympathetic ears, not pills. An opinion poll in the UK showed that 92 per cent of the British public were in favour of counselling rather than pills as a treatment.

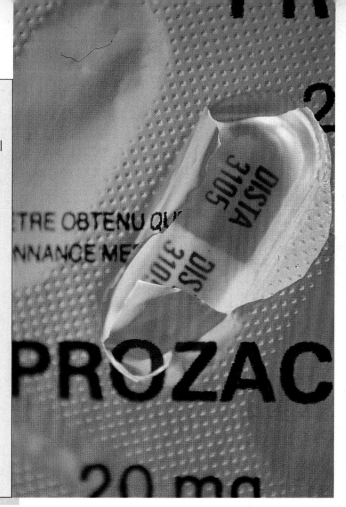

Herbal remedies

For those who don't want to take traditional antidepressants, a more natural remedy can be found in herbal medicine. St. John's wort, also known as hypericum, grows throughout Europe. In tablet form it is now widely used in Germany, where it is prescribed 20 times more often than other antidepressants for cases of mild depression.

'Plastic surgery for the personality' is one description of the drug Prozac (above), one of the newest forms of antidepressants known as SSRIs.

Drugs (left) are frequently prescribed in the treatment of mental illness, but not everyone is in favour of their use.

Depression is not the only problem that can benefit from medication. Its opposite extremes, mania and manic depression, often have to be treated with mood-stabilising drugs, in particular lithium. Kidney problems can occur if the level of lithium in the blood is too high, so its uses must be monitored.

Experts, doctors and users themselves are divided over the use of such drugs. Supporters say that, despite the side-effects, powerful drugs, such as those now used for schizophrenia, give the majority of sufferers a fair quality of life which they would probably not enjoy without their use. They can't cure, but they can control the symptoms. Others believe that drugs may be over-used as 'liquid coshes' to keep sufferers quiet and controlled.

Case study

Modern medication can transform the lives of people who would once have had no opportunity of leading anything like a normal life. Mahadev was diagnosed with schizophrenia in his early twenties. That was 20 years ago and since then he's been in hospital six times. The first time, he was given doses of powerful drugs with side-effects which made him feel completely numbed. 'I couldn't connect to anybody or anything, I didn't recognize my parents or my sister when they visited me. I was like a zombie. it was a horrible experience.'

Today Mahadev has a steady job as a bus driver and enjoys spending time with his two children and wife. He says his success is due to 'great family and friends' and his medication; very different now to the drugs he was given 20 years ago. He takes three different drugs plus a monthly injection.

Members of the National Schizophrenia Fellowship drop-in centre in London enjoy the company and conversation.

Talking it through

Often, people who take drugs to treat mental illnesses, such as depression or anxiety, have counselling or psychotherapy too. Medication is usually used first to help lift the mood, and then the sufferer feels more confident talking about his or her problems. Sometimes, if a person is suffering from only mild depression, counselling or psychotherapy can be used on its own.

Counsellors help people by listening, helping them explore their feelings, but they don't always analyse or give out advice. A good counsellor is like a good friend, but a friend who doesn't make judgements or interfere. An increasing number of GPs have counsellors working at their surgeries.

Talking problems through with a psychotherapist can help an individual to understand the reasons for his or her distress.

There are several types of psychotherapy available for individuals, families or groups. Psychotherapy or counselling can be provided by psychiatrists, nurses, social workers or psychologists. A psychotherapist works by helping the sufferer to look at problems in a fresh way. They might enable someone to discover something from the past that lies at the heart of their unhappiness and help them understand why they feel as they do. They may also help draw up a plan of action to reduce these negative or distressing feelings. One of the most successful therapies is called Cognitive Behavioural Therapy, which works by teaching people to replace negative thoughts with something more positive and helpful. Unfortunately, psychotherapy can prove expensive, and it is quite scarce and so much in demand that there may be a wait of months before seeing a therapist.

The way we are today

According to the mental health charity MIND, in its 50th Anniversary report in 1996, 50 years ago the majority of people using psychiatric services in England were in-patients in psychiatric hospitals. Today just a quarter are in-patients. Whenever possible, in the developed world, people with mental health problems are seen as out-patients – at home, in the doctor's surgery, or at psychiatric clinics or community mental health centres. Often, people in other areas of the world are not so lucky.

Hospital care

There are times when admission to hospital is seen as the best solution for a patient. A psychiatric 'emergency', such as a sudden shock, like an unexpected bereavement, may cause an individual to suffer acute distress and be unable to cope without help; a mental health problem may cause self-neglect (failure to eat, wash etc.) or self-harm (over-use of alcohol or drugs, attempted suicide); or someone's behaviour may

Sometimes admission to hospital is the best solution for cases of acute mental illness, when overwhelming distress can lead to self-harm or suicide.

become so disturbing that the people around him or her cannot cope. Sometimes such people have to be taken to hospital against their will. It is important to understand that today most people are admitted to hospital informally and are free to leave when they wish.

For the homeless, life on the streets is bleak and hopeless. Mental health problems and physical illness often remain untreated.

Homelessness

According to a World Mental Health report in 1995, there are nearly 20 million refugees in the world today, plus another 20 million who have been forced to leave their homes within their own countries. Many suffer from mental problems, yet the sort of medical services and treatment offered in the West are unheard of for them. One Palestinian woman told a reporter, 'If I would sit down and start to think of my feelings I could break down. You, the Europeans, can enjoy the luxury of analysing your feelings. We simply have to endure.'

A caring community?

The idea of community care (where patients were permitted to live in the community) for the seriously mentally ill was developed in the 1960s, initially in the United States. The idea then spread to Europe and countries such as Canada and Australia. It was a reaction against the old-style mental hospitals, or asylums, where the emphasis was on custody rather than care or cure. Many people lived for long periods in these bleak establishments and became apathetic and increasingly dependent on them – 'institutionalized'.

Schemes allowing patients to live in the community can mean life on the streets for mentally ill people who are discharged from hospital, and don't have friends or relatives.

The combination of more humane attitudes – a belief that the mentally ill had a right to care in their homes, not just in hospital – together with improvements in medication, led to the gradual closure of many, though not all, of these huge asylums. They were replaced by smaller psychiatric wards in general hospitals and mental health centres.

Life can be hard for those people who find themselves living in a dingy room or hostel when they have to leave hospital.

A good idea but . . .

Unfortunately, although most people in the developed world continue to support the idea of community care in principle, in practice it has had many failings and these have led to widespread criticism. The most common complaints are that community care has not been properly researched and planned, and has been starved of financial resources. The

overall result, say critics, is that the majority of mentally ill patients, many of them suffering from schizophrenia and manic depression, have been released into a community without the means to care for themselves. Governments have been accused of cynically using community care as a way of reducing the cost of treating people with mental illness.

Who cares?

The realities of community care for many of those experiencing it – amongst them many of the most vulnerable members of society – can be life in a dingy room or hostel, or even homelessness. The lack of beds has meant that some patients have to be sent out of hospital to make way for others, when it is clear that they are still unwell.

Hospital-based care

Russia still operates a fully hospital-based system of caring for the mentally ill. Conditions there highlight what was wrong with the old institutional care in the West and what led to the schemes where patients were allowed to live in the community. The Kashenko Hospital in Moscow has the capacity for 7,000 in-patients and 5,000 staff, mainly unqualified nurses. Wards contain up to 40 beds with no private space, and are very cold, as heating is expensive. Sanitation is poor and all wards are locked. Yet psychiatric and welfare services outside the hospital are virtually non-existent, so residents would be even worse off in the community.

From *Mental Health in Europe* by Shulamit Ramon (1996)

Research shows that many people living rough also suffer from mental health problems and may even take their own lives when their situation seems most desperate.

Fear in the community

Most people's knowledge of schemes that allow patients to live in the community comes mainly from media reports about killings and assaults on members of the public by mentally ill people. In 1997, a British survey showed that, on average, one murder every two weeks was committed by mental patients released from hospital. Some of these patients had discharged themselves from hospital against-medical advice and others had failed to take their prescribed medicine. These were patients suffering from serious mental illness. Yet statistics also show that most mental health patients (particularly those with schizophrenia or manic depression) harm themselves rather than other people. The risk of suicide is very high amongst people discharged after treatment.

Protecting the community

But there are some safeguards designed to protect the community and the patient. From 1994, in the UK, the Department of Health has required all health authorities to identify people thought to be at risk of harming themselves or others, by putting their names on a supervision register. Many countries also now insist that released patients must have a 'care keyworker' to keep an eye on them, plus a home to go to and a plan for their care. Unfortunately, staff and money shortages, as well as poor liaison between psychiatric departments, has meant that people still don't always get the care they need, and the community is still not protected.

Having someone to talk to and keep an eye on you is vital when you have a mental illness such as schizophrenia, as this man discovers.

Case study

It's easy to become almost invisible when you are mentally vulnerable and have no family or friends to watch out for you. Mario's mother died when he was 12. 'She just drank herself to death,' he says. 'I found her dead on her bed just before Christmas.'

That was 15 years ago. Mario's father had long since left home and he lived with his grandmother for a short time: 'But she couldn't cope with me.' Since then Mario has tried to commit suicide 14 times, spent two years living rough on the streets and had two stays in hospital. He wishes he could return there sometimes. 'I felt so safe there,' he says. Instead he lives in a one-room flat where he spends his time watching TV and smoking. Two or three times a week he goes to a day centre run by a national charity and has a hot meal and a game of cards. 'People who are not mentally ill don't care about us,' he says. 'I know that I'm ill, but I'm not getting any help or support and have got no one to turn to. The only thing people like me have got is this centre. People think we're dangerous and that we will go out and kill someone, but I wouldn't hurt a fly. The only thing that I've ever hurt is myself.' And Mario rolls up his sleeves and shows the scars on his forearms.

Hospital may be the safest place for some severely mentally ill people who could harm themselves or others, but should people be forced to go to hospital against their will?

Two-sided story

In 1997, a controversial TV programme filmed at a London psychiatric hospital interviewed a doctor who called for it to be made easier to section (certify) potentially dangerous mentally ill people. He suggested that they should be brought into hospital and, in some cases, should be forced to have injections, to ensure that patients continue their medication. He said that there was always an element of risk when mentally ill people were released into the community. The risk, he said, could not be eliminated, it could only be kept to a minimum. It is no easy thing to ensure the freedom of the person who is ill, but at the same time protect the general public from any risk. Some people believe that forcing a person into hospital would be an attack on their civil liberties, others think it would 'save' them (and the community) from their potentially violent actions.

The controversy over what should constitute good care in the community continues to grow. In the UK in January 1998, care in the community was criticized by the government, who promised to protect the public – and patients themselves – by providing more supervised residential units.

Keeping it in the family

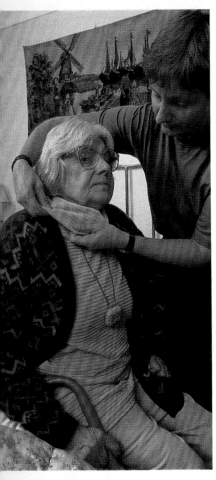

They looked after you when you were a child, now they need looking after in the same way. Caring for a granny who may have forgotten how to dress herself is just one of the caring roles undertaken by some families.

When we talk about people suffering with a mental illness, mild or severe, we are usually referring to the individuals who have the illness. But there are other sufferers, people who don't have an illness themselves but who have to live with its effects – the families and friends of the disturbed individuals.

Across the world there are ordinary people with no special skills or training, caring for someone with a mental health problem. They come from all walks of life, and many different cultural, religious and ethnic backgrounds. Their circumstances will vary depending on their income, the severity of the mental health problem and the outside help and support available in the locality. Some carers are elderly, some only children themselves.

What shall we do?

The sort of situations families have to face when confronting mental illness can be extremely distressing. What does it feel like when a husband suddenly refuses to talk to his wife because voices tell him she's not really his wife? What does it feel like when your brother turns up on the doorstep, dirty and distressed, and threatens to kill himself? What does a small child feel like when his mother won't let him play with friends because she believes an evil spirit will attack him if he leaves the house? What does it feel like when a grandparent can't remember who you are or even how to dress him-or herself?

All these and similar situations are part of the experiences of those 'caring' for a person with mental problems. This caring can be so demanding that the carer's own needs are overlooked or forgotten, and families are in danger of splitting up. Some carers have to admit that they cannot cope. It is not uncommon for elderly people to have to go into a nursing home. They become a risk if they start wandering around the house during the night, switching on cookers and fires, or going out of the house alone, unaware of where they are going.

A family affair

Families looking after someone with a mental illness have to face stigma. 'My mum's schizophrenic and I've looked after her and my two young brothers since I was eight, when dad left home,' says Rachael, now 17. 'I've seen her through four overdoses and repeated stays in hospital, but the only one of us she ever put to any harm was herself. People like mum need support and understanding. I love my mum and I've never resented looking after her.'

Children care

The children's charity Barnardo's estimates that about 30 per cent of all children who look after parents and support their families are caring for a parent who is mentally ill.

If a parent is mentally ill children may have to care for him or her, or look after their sisters and brothers.

Talking point

'The large number of people in households in developing countries means that there is a network of people who can share the responsibility for the patient's care and recovery. There is a strong sense of duty and they all share the burden.'

Professor Julian Leff of the Institute of Psychiatry in London, addressing a meeting of the Royal College of Psychiatrists in 1996.

Do you feel that families have a 'duty' to care for the seriously mentally ill? Do you think that those families and individuals who do the 'caring' do so out of love and duty or because they have no choice?

We're all here to help

In Western countries, caring for family members, especially those who are ill, is not as common as it is in the East, where extended family networks are still the norm. In India, in particular, family members play an active role in caring for mentally ill members of their family. Unlike Europe and the United States, where the family is often thought of as part of the patient's problem, the Indian family is seen as part of the solution. Family members are expected to help provide therapy for the patient and to take responsibility for his or her cure.

Family involvement is rooted in Indian culture, which insists that someone other than the sick person makes a decision about care. Once the family has decided that a person needs treatment, a family member is chosen to oversee the care. He or she brings the patient to see the doctor, receives prescriptions and makes sure the patient follows the doctor's orders. Some may stay with the patient in hospital or go in every day to look after his or her practical needs.

Asian families are usually very close-knit, so that if a member of the group becomes mentally ill, everyone is expected to help.

Different lives

But what happens when people from countries such as India move to countries in the West? A study by the Mental Health Foundation in 1955 revealed that Asians tended to have lower rates of mental illness overall than the white population, although they appeared to have a higher rate of schizophrenia. A reason given for this was that the Asian community, even when living in another country, had genuinely low rates of mental illness because of its family support system. Attitudes may have changed as Asian families have become more westernized and lost their community outlook. But it was also suggested that there might be a reluctance among members of ethnic groups to approach mental health services, either because of language difficulties, or the fear of stigma or being diagnosed as having a psychotic illness. A fear of discrimination might also be a cause. In the UK, the junior health minister said that young black people regard mental health services as off-limits, because they fear being diagnosed schizophrenic, put on sedatives and forced to go into hospital.

Members of some ethnic groups may not get help when they are suffering from mental illness because of language barriers, or a fear of racial discrimination.

Taking your life

When someone commits suicide it has a devastating effect on the family and friends, who have to come to terms with their dreadful loss. Many will need support and counselling to help them cope with the situation. Every year, more than 1.5 million people throughout the world commit suicide, and the rate for attempted suicide is thought to be ten to twenty times higher. Many people seriously injure themselves, sometimes permanently, without succeeding in killing themselves. The importance of a supportive family and friends is emphasized by the fact that the highest suicide rates, according to the experts, are those in societies where family ties are weak and there's no sense of community.

When the future seems hopeless and out of control, and the next drink is never far away, suicide may seem the only solution to the really desperate.

Reaching the limit

When someone takes his or her life there are many personal reasons behind the action – it may be a reaction to a distressing event or severe disappointment, an expression of hopelessness about the future, an angry gesture or an escape from intolerable stresses and problems, real or imagined.

Who is at risk?

There is a higher-than-average suicide rate among people with mental illnesses such as severe depression, manic depression and schizophrenia. Social isolation and lack of support make these people particularly vulnerable. Alcoholics are also at risk – 15 per cent of them commit suicide every year, and drug users are 20 per cent more likely to kill themselves than non-users.

Dying young

Suicide amongst the young is a trend that, sadly, seems to be increasing every year. It's now among the top two or three causes of death in the under - 25s in many countries of the world – New Zealand has the highest suicide rate for young men. In the UK, where suicide was a criminal offence until 1961, over 5,000 people kill themselves every year. In the United States the suicide toll is even more alarming, with 30,000 suicides a year, 80 per cent of them men.

Talking through your troubles can help, but the demands of life today have caused an increase in the suicide rate for young people worldwide.

Pressure to learn

Suicides are on the increase in South Korea, and school pressure (studying for up to 17 hours a day) was thought to have been a factor in the 191 suicides among children of school age in the early 1990s.

Is it getting better?

People recovering from a spell of mental illness, however severe or mild, have the same goals as those recovering from a physical illness or accident – to get back on their feet and get on with their lives. Their requirements are the same as anybody else's – money to live on (preferably from a job), decent housing, friends and a reasonable quality of life. Relying on medical treatment isn't enough – the practical problems need attention, too.

Getting a job can help you get back on your feet when you're recovering from a mental illness.

Unfortunately, one of the effects of mental illness is that a sufferer loses the ability to cope with everyday life, and this can lead to serious problems with money, employment and housing. These problems themselves produce more tension and worry, which in their turn cause further mental distress and stand in the way of recovery.

Just the job

A job, of course, is not just about money in your pocket. It offers purpose, contact with other people, status, a feeling of usefulness and it is good for self-esteem – something which those suffering from a mental illness tend to lose. For some people recovering from milder forms of mental illness, such as depression, getting a full-time job is a priority. People who have more serious problems, such as schizophrenia, may never have worked or may be unable to work full time. For these people, a more realistic first step may be of learning new skills and self-confidence in a sheltered setting.

Prejudice at work

Finding suitable work when you have suffered any form of mental illness is extremely difficult. It is often said by people who have suffered from mental illness that once you have a history of mental health problems your chances of getting a good job again are virtually non-existent. Often they are forced to take jobs with much less responsibility than they were given before. One occupational psychologist said: 'Always appear well-balanced and psychologically stable at job interviews. Never admit to even minor nervous symptoms.'

Having a job means having money to go out with friends and re-establish a social life – vital when recovering from a mental illness. Work and friends are very important.

Prejudices and discrimination

In many countries employers can search records to see if potential employees have had mental problems in the past. This, it is said, enables employers to decide how likely someone is to have a relapse. This often leads to discrimination and prevents those with a history of mental illness from getting a job.

Are we being fair?

Employers' responses to those with mental illness only mirror those of the general public. A survey conducted for the BBC in 1995 revealed that only one in 20 people believed a person with a mental illness should be allowed a responsible job such as a doctor, nurse, or police officer. However, almost half of the 2,000 people interviewed thought the mentally ill were very well qualified to be actors or comedians!

One man, with an obsessive/compulsive disorder, admitted lying to get work on two occasions. 'I said my two-and-a-half-year absence from employment was due to a term spent in prison. I was accepted for the first job and short-listed for the second. Whenever I have been truthful about my psychiatric past, I have never been accepted for a job.'

If you admit that you have been mentally ill you could lose the chance of a good job. The law may be able to help you in such cases of discrimination.

Lost time

Calculations made in the UK in 1997 estimated that mental health problems cost the UK around £32 billion a year. This includes the cost of lost employment, social security payments and treatment costs. In the United States, calculations made in 1994 estimated that $40 billion are drained each year from the United States in lost working hours.

Work itself can be very stressful. Mental illness is one of the major reasons for absences from work.

Fair deal

The new Disability Discrimination Act, introduced in the UK in 1997, may help some of those people suffering with a mental illness to get a fairer deal. It makes it unlawful for an employer to refuse to hire a job applicant, or to sack a worker, because of a disability, without good reason. In the United States, which has a similar law, the largest category of claims against employers feature mental illnesses such as depression. In Sweden there is legislation to stop employers bullying vulnerable employees and causing them stress.

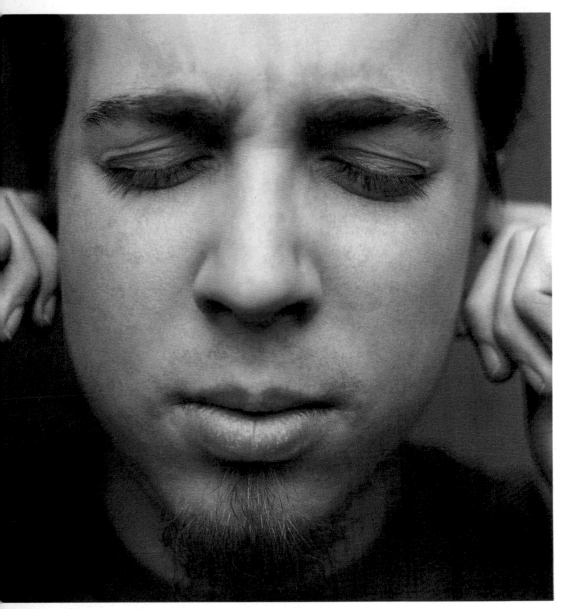

Some people just don't want to hear or speak about mental illness, but celebrities from the world of film, television and music are often quite outspoken about their own experiences.

Star treatment

Fortunately not everyone is blinkered by prejudice about mental illness. Many celebrities have now publicly discussed the mental problems they, or members of their families, have experienced. According to Michael Palin, whose sister killed herself: 'Often people with a mental illness are wrongly labelled and we never take time to find out what lies behind the labels. All it takes to make life better for them is a change in attitudes.' Singer Janet Jackson has told how she had a breakdown, from which she recovered, in 1995. 'But the last three years have been the darkest of my life. I've felt depressed to a frightening level,' she said in 1997.

Speaking out

Actress Joanna Lumley had a breakdown when she was 24. 'I went into a real black hole. I don't know what triggered it off. I suppose it was fear,' she has explained. Comedian Spike Milligan suffers with manic depression. 'What I suffer from is the great invisible illness. It puts me on my back. It saps me of all physical energy and my mind goes into neutral. I can think of five occasions when I thought I'd commit suicide.' And finally, among those celebrities who are said to have taken Prozac to cope with depression are actors Al Pacino and Jim Carey, actress Roseanne Arnold, the Duchess of York and the late Diana, Princess of Wales (for bulimia).

The fact that all of these famous people have felt able to talk openly about their various experiences with mental illness shows that there cannot be as much stigma as there has been in the past, but are their illnesses acceptable purely because they are famous?

Bulimia

Describing the bulimia which she even suffered from on her honeymoon on the Royal Yacht Britannia with Prince Charles, Diana said: "Appalling, absolutely appalling. It was rife, four times a day on the yacht. Anything I could find I would gobble up and then I would be sick two minutes later. I was very tired. So, of course, that slightly got the mood swings going in the sense that one minute I would be happy, the next blubbing. I cried my eyes out on my honeymoon. . .'

Diana, Princess of Wales, was open and forthright about her battle with bulimia, the eating disorder.

Mind games – keeping mentally fit

Fit for life

With all the stresses, strains and pressures of life today, it's not easy to keep our mental health in top condition at all times. But there are ways of preparing yourself for when the going gets tough. Strange as it may seem, keeping well physically plays a big part – there's a lot of truth in that old saying about 'a healthy mind in a healthy body'.

Make sure you eat well, and regularly, and remember that too many caffeine-loaded drinks, like coffee and fizzy drinks, can make you feel anxious and irritable. And alcohol? It may make people appear as if they're having a good time but, despite popular opinion, it's a depressant which will only make you feel good for a short while before it makes you feel much worse.

Exercise doesn't have to be in the gym or on the games field, it doesn't have to cost anything and it needn't be competitive. It's relaxing and can be a

Exercise can do just as much for your mental and emotional well-being as it will for your physical strength and stamina.

real help if your worries stop you from winding down and sleeping properly. Your mind is better able to sort out problems while you're on the move, and the exercise will make you physically tired. And, a big plus, exercise will not only make you feel better but look better – and when you look good, you tend to feel good about yourself. Now that creates a healthy circle.

Learn how to switch off. That sounds as if it should be easy, but for many people it's not, they have to be taught how to unwind. You can go to relaxation classes, or take up yoga or meditation. Or you can read a book, see a film, paint a picture, talk to friends, anything that slows you down and switches your mind off work and worries.

Laugh it off

Laughter is still one of the best medicines, according to stress consultant Robert Holden, who established the first ever Laughter Clinic in the UK. 'Since the 1950s, in particular, well over 500 medical research papers have been published on the potential medicinal worth of mirth.' In India, one holy man ran a retreat, or ashram, where he got his followers to laugh for three hours and then cry for three hours. This was said to have a very therapeutic effect.

Best of friends

Someone to talk to and have a laugh with – a close friend or relative you trust – can be invaluable when you are feeling anxious or depressed. Keeping problems to yourself is not a good idea, whether you are ten or fifty. Old sayings like 'a problem shared is a problem halved' have a lot of sense in them.

Enjoying a joke with a group of friends will help you relax and take your mind off your worries. Being able to switch off is vital when you feel under pressure and strain.

Telling it like it is

But if you feel you can't confide in any friends, or feel you haven't any friends or understanding relatives to turn to with a problem, don't suffer in isolation. Seek help from your doctor if you feel there is something wrong. You certainly won't be alone – around one in eight people go to their family doctor every year to talk about emotional problems. Remember, it is far better to get help early if you need it, than to wait until things are really bad.

Caring for children

Child psychotherapist Trudy Klauber said that 'Childhood depression which becomes chronic may be reactivated throughout life. The child who is helped through a depression and feels cared about may gain strength from the experience.'

Talking about your feelings always helps.

Organizations like MIND, SANE, the American National Alliance for the Mentally Ill (NAMI) and self-help groups such as Depressives Anonymous can also help if you have a mental health problem and need advice or someone to talk to. Nowadays experts are beginning to take mental illnesses such as depression very seriously in young people.

Out in the open

Providing information in schools is now seen as vital in promoting a positive approach to mental health issues. 'In a world where family and job security are decreasing, school offers an important environment in which to encourage the good mental health of young people,' a spokesman said in 1997, on the launch of MIND's mental health education project.

Planning for health

In the UK government's Health of the Nation Plan in 1992, five key areas, including mental health, were named as targets for improvement by the year 2000. The aims were to improve significantly the health and social functioning of mentally ill people; to reduce the overall suicide rate by 15 per cent; and to reduce the suicide rate of severely mentally ill people by at least 33 per cent.

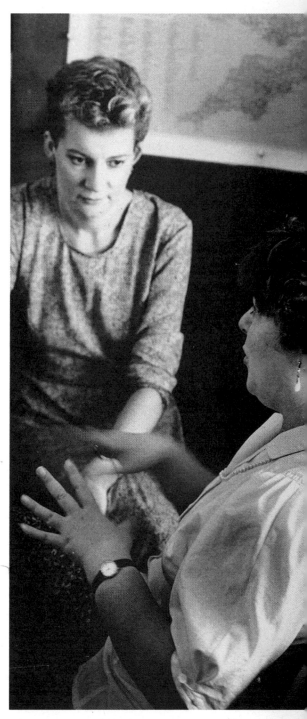

If you have a mental health problem and want to discuss it, there are many organizations to give you advice.

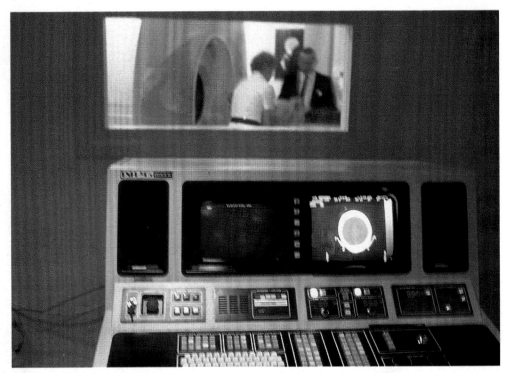

Hope for the future?

In 1990, the USA's Congress announced a $2 billion per year programme to 'map the mind', effectively funding a massive drug research campaign. As a result, it's expected that a whole new class of drugs, each homing in on a specific brain molecule, is being developed for the future. It's been suggested that these 'made to order' spirit-raisers will make it possible to adjust anyone's brain chemistry and modify their behaviour.

Spotting potential problems with the aid of a brain scan could help doctors to help people with a mental illness, possibly before it becomes too severe.

And in another twenty years, doctors will be able to spot all sorts of potential problems just by looking at the brain. Asked to predict their vision of psychiatry in 2020, two specialists, Dr Mary Phillips and Dr Steve Williams, said that they expected to be able to scan a brain and pick out any problem areas – difficulty in controlling anger, tendency to anxiety – just from the pictures.

Looking forward

DNA technology will also soon be able to offer screening tests for diseases such as Alzheimer's disease. However, this sort of genetic testing is viewed with apprehension by many experts who feel that, until effective treatment is available, telling someone of 20 that they are likely to develop a disease at 60 does more harm than good.

Where most experts do agree is that little progress will be made now, or in the future, until we all begin to understand the real pain and distress that mental illness causes worldwide.

Being able to discuss mental illness without embarrassment or prejudice is vital now, and will be in future years.

Talking point

'Drug companies must be allowed to research into drugs capable of restoring the minds of those facing dementia, depression or insanity. But we must be on our guard against the siren call of "miracle" drugs that promise to improve us all. For that way, madness lies.'

Writer Robert Matthews in the *Daily Express*, 1996.

Should drugs which act against conditions such as depression and anxiety be more readily available, so that all of us could be happy all the time and unhappiness become non-existent?

Glossary

Agoraphobia A fear of being in public places that causes anxiety and a desire to avoid such places.

Alcohol dependence (alcoholism) Repeated abuse of alcohol.

Alzheimer's disease A form of dementia which develops slowly.

Anorexia nervosa A disorder in which sufferers starve themselves to avoid weight gain.

Antidepressant drugs Drugs that help lift depression.

Anxiety The group of feelings that occur at times of acute stress.

Asylum Literally, a place of safety. In the past the word was used to describe psychiatric institutions.

Behaviour therapy An 'action cure' in which a therapist, usually a clinical psychologist, helps a patient to examine problem behaviour patterns and change them for the better.

Bulimia nervosa A psychological disorder in which the sufferer secretly has huge eating binges then makes him or herself vomit. Also, sufferers may use laxatives to avoid weight gain.

Chronic illness A long illness. The term does not relate to severity.

Cognitive therapy A kind of mental 'retraining' in positive rather than negative thinking which is common when ill.

Community care Continuing care outside hospital for people who would otherwise need to live in hospital.

Community mental health centre A facility like a GP centre, catering solely for people with mental health problems.

Compulsion An unwelcome urge to perform a certain action.

Counselling One kind of 'talking cure' in which people are given the chance to explore their feelings and find personal and practical solutions to their problems.

Delusion A belief or idea that is false, not explained by the person's past experiences and cannot be shaken by logical argument. Occurs in psychotic illnesses like schizophrenia and manic depression.

Depression A feeling of deep unhappiness that lasts for a long while and stops sufferers from getting on with their lives.

Drug Any chemical, whether natural or artificial, taken for some specific effect.

Electroconvulsive therapy (ECT) Treatment in which a small electric current is passed through the brain of an anaesthetised and relaxed patient (usually someone with severe depression) to induce a fit and alleviate psychiatric symptoms.

Gene A chemical in your body that defines your body's appearance and function – and passes on characteristics to the next generation.

Hallucination An experience of one of the five senses (hearing, vision, taste, smell, touch) which is perceived as real but has no external cause.

Learning disabilities Intellectual impairment starting early in life, usually before or around the time of birth. People with learning disabilities were previously called mentally handicapped.

Lithium A drug used to stabilise mood swings and alleviate mania and severe depression.

Mania Being excited and energetic in a way that goes beyond normal happiness, accompanied by restlessness, irritability and psychosis.

Neurotic disorders Psychiatric disorders in which the symptoms are like exaggerations of normal experience and the patient does not lose touch with reality.

Obsession A thought or pattern of behaviour that occurs repeatedly, for no obvious reason, and causes anxiety.

Panic attack When anxiety occurs suddenly and severely.

Paranoia Has a wide range of meanings in the history of psychiatry but is now used to describe strong feelings or delusions of persecution.

Psychiatrist Medical doctor who has trained and specialised in psychiatry.

Psychoanalysis A kind of psychotherapy in which the therapist interprets the client or patient's problems. Often this is based on one or another school of mental philosophy, such as that of Freud or Jung.

Psychologist A non-medical specialist with a degree in psychology.

Psychology The social science that studies human behaviour.

Psychosurgery Operating on the brain to alleviate severe psychiatric illness or very troublesome personality traits. Rarely performed now

Psychotic depression A severe form of depression with psychotic features, such as hallucinations and delusions.

Recreational drug use Using drugs such as LSD , Ecstasy or marijuana for non-medical reasons, primarily to gain a particular effect such as relaxation or intense pleasure.

Sectioning Under the British Mental Health Act of 1983 a disturbed patient who refuses to accept psychiatric help can be sectioned, meaning that the patient is forced to go into hospital to receive treatment.

Self-harm A non-fatal act such as a drug overdose or wrist cutting. Has the same meaning as parasuicide.

Serotonin A chemical message in the brain, thought to be lacking in people with depression.

Books to Read

Facts about Alzheimer's Disease by Laurie Beckelman, Crestwood House, 1996.

Facts About Fears and Phobias by Renardo Barden, Crestwood House, 1989.

Dealing With: Substance Abuse by J.Coleman and Y. Solomon, Wayland, 1995.

Face the Facts: Diet and Health by Alison Dalgleish, Wayland, 1997.

Nothing to be Ashamed of: Growing Up with Mental Illness in Your Family by Sherry H. Dinner, Lothrop, Lee and Shepard Books, 1989.

Alzheimer's Disease: The Silent Epidemic by Julie Frank, Lerner Publications, 1985.

Emotional Illness in Your Family: Helping Your Relative, Helping Yourself by Harvey Roy Greenberg, Macmillan, 1989.

Talking Points: Alcohol by Emma Haughton, Wayland, 1998.

Dealing With: Stress by Emma Haughton, Wayland, 1995.

Dealing With: Eating Disorders by Kate Haycock, Wayland, 1995.

My Grammy: A Book About Alzheimer's Disease by Marsha Kibbey, Carolrhoda books, 1988.

When Food's a Foe: How to Confront and Conquer Eating Disorders by Nancy L. Kolodney, Boston, Little, Brown, 1992.

Face the Facts: Drugs by Adrian King, Wayland, 1997.

What Do You Know About? Depression and Mental Health by Pete Sanders and Steve Myers, Watts, 1996

Living With a Parent Who Takes Drugs by Judith S. Seixas, Greenwillow Books, 1989.

Talking Points: Homelessness by Kaye Stearman, Wayland, 1998.

Suitable for older readers

Closing the Asylum by Peter Barham, Penguin, 1997.

Young People Under Stress by Sally Burningham, Virago, 1994.

Who Can I Talk To? The User's Guide to Therapy and Counselling by Judy Cooper and Jenny Lewis, Headway, 1995.

World Mental Health: Problems and Priorities in Low-Income Countries by Robert Desjarlais, Leon Eisenberg, Bryon Good, Arthur Kleinman, Oxford University Press, 1996.

Depression by Jack Dominian, Fontana, 1990.

The Mental Health Handbook by Tony Drew and Madeleine King, Piatkus, 1995.

Mental Health, Race and Culture by Suman Fernando, MacMillan, 1991.

The Consumer Guide to Mental Health by Dr Trish Groves and Dr Ian Pennell, Harper Collins, 1995.

One Flew Over the Cuckoo's Nest by Ken Kesey, Picador, 1988.

Living with Schizophrenia by Dr Brenda Lintner, Optima, 1995.

Depression and How to Survive It by Spike Milligan and Dr Anthony Clare, Arrow, 1994.

A Social History of Madness by Roy Porter, Phoenix Giant, 1996.

Mental Health in Europe by Shulamit Ramon, MacMillan, 1996.

Overcoming Panic by Derrick Silove and Vijaya Manicavasagar, Robinson Publishing, 1997.

Useful Addresses

African Caribbean Mental Health Initiative
35-37 Electric Avenue, Brixton
London, SW9 8JP

Alzheimer's Disease Society, Gordon House,
10 Greencoat Place, London, SW1P 1PH
Telephone: 0171 306 0606

Anti-Bullying Campaign,
185 Tower Bridge Road, London, SE1 2UF
Telephone: 0171 378 1446

British Association for Counselling
1 Regent Place, Rugby, CV21 2PJ
Telephone: 01788 550899

Children's Legal Centre
University of Essex, Wivenhoe Park
Colchester, Essex, CO4 3SQ
Advice line: 01206 873820

Depression Alliance
35 Westminster Bridge Road
London, SE1 7JB
Telephone: 0171 633 9929

Drinkline
Petersham House, 54a Hatton Garden
London, EC1N 8HP
Telephone: 0171 520 5303
Helpline: 0345 320202

Drugline
9a Brockley Cross,
London, SE4 2AB
Telephone: 0181 692 4975

Eating Disorders Association
First Floor, Wensum House
103 Prince of Wales Road
Norwich, NR1 1TW
Telephone: 01603 6211414

Headlines: Mental Health Media
The Resource Centre, 256 Holloway Road
London, N7 6PA
Telephone: 0171 700 8129

Manic Depression Fellowship
8–10 High Street, Kingston Upon Thames
Surrey, KT1 1SS
Telephone: 0181 974 6550

Mental After Care Association (MACA)
25 Bedford Square
London, SW1B 3HW
Telephone: 0171 436 6194

Mental Health Foundation
37 Mortimer Street, London, W1N 8JU
Telephone: 0171 580 0145

Mind
Granta House, 15–19 Broadway
Stratford, London, E15 4BQ
Telephone: 0181 519 2122

Muslim Information Centre
233 Seven Sisters Road,
London, N4 2DA
Telephone: 0171 272 5170

National Schizophrenia Fellowship
28 Castle Street, Kingston upon Thames
Surrey, KT1 1SS
Advice line: 0181 974 6814

Samaritans
10 The Grove, Slough, SL1 1QP
Telephone: 01753 532713
Helpline: 0345 909090

Saneline
2nd Floor, 199–205 Old Marylebone Road
London, NW1 5QP
Helpline: 0171 724 6570
Telephone: 01345 678000

Young Minds
102–108 Clerkenwell Road
London, EC1M 5SA
Telephone: 0171 336 8445

USA

American Association for Counselling and
International Association of Counselling
Services Inc., 599 Stevenson Avenue,
Alexandria, VA22304

The League Treatment Center (for mentally
handicapped children and adults)
30 Washington St.
Brooklyn, NY 11201
Telephone: 800 6768008

Steinway Child and Family Service (mental
health services)
41–36 27th Street, Long Island City
NY 11101
Telephone: 718 3895100

Index